ENGLAND'S
— WORLD —
HERITAGE

BY JOHN HEDGECOE

ENGLISH HERITAGE

1 3 5 7 9 8 6 4 2

British Library Cataloguing-in-Publication Data:
A catalogue record for this book is available from the British Library.

ISBN 1 85585 488 0 (hardback)
ISBN 1 85585 489 9 (paperback)

Conceived, edited and designed by
Collins & Brown Ltd

Editorial Director: Colin Ziegler
Editor: Robin Gurdon
Art Director for English Heritage: John Hedgecoe
Designer: Claire Graham
Photographic Assistant: Jenny Mackintosh

Reproduced in Great Britain by Reed Reprographics, Ipswich
Printed and bound in Great Britain by Jarrold's, Thetford

All photographs are the copyright of English Heritage except the
following which are reproduced by kind permission of the National
Trust: Front cover; 6–7 (below centre, below right and above right);
74–5 (all); 76–7 (all); 78 (above left); 89; 90–1.

COVER *Hadrian's Wall crosses the bleak and open landscape of
northern England at Hotbank Crag.*

BACK COVER *The Galilee, or Lady Chapel, of Durham Cathedral is
adorned with exuberant zig-zag carving.*

TITLE PAGE *The coffered ceiling of the magnificent Chapel of the
Royal Naval Hospital at Greenwich.*

CONTENTS

HADRIAN'S WALL

DURHAM

FOUNTAINS ABBEY

IRONBRIDGE

BLENHEIM PALACE

AVEBURY

WESTMINSTER
TOWER OF LONDON

GREENWICH

BATH
STONEHENGE

CANTERBURY

FOREWORD

THIS BOOK CELEBRATES THE magnificence of England's World Heritage. The photographs by John Hedgecoe and the words by David Souden take us from the majestic uplands of Hadrian's Wall to the packed terraces of Georgian Bath, and from the great fortress the Tower of London to the rural seclusion of Fountains Abbey and Studley Royal.

Together, the ten sites encapsulate many of England's contributions to the world's heritage. The stone circles and earthworks of Stonehenge and Avebury show the skill and power of our prehistoric ancestors in moulding their landscape and marking their beliefs, while Canterbury marks the reintroduction of Christianity to southern Britain 1,400 years ago.

Durham demonstrates the superlative architectural triumphs of the medieval church. Bath epitomises a talent for gracious urban living.

Blenheim Palace and its park are an elegant memory of military might given by a grateful nation to John, first Duke of Marlborough. The Palace of Westminster and Westminster Abbey are the living embodiment of our national pride. Greenwich, nominated but not yet inscribed as the eleventh English World Heritage Site, is the greatest collection of historic buildings in the country. Ironbridge is the birthplace of the Industrial Revolution which has transformed the world over the last 250 years.

English Heritage is publishing this book on England's World Heritage to mark the 25th Anniversary of the adoption of the World Heritage Convention by UNESCO on 16th November 1972.

The Convention was part of the international response to the pace of destruction of the world's natural and cultural heritage after the Second World War. Following on from the successful international efforts to rescue the Abu Simbel and Philae temples in Egypt, the Convention recognised that some of our heritage is so significant that it forms a world heritage of 'outstanding universal value ... for whose protection it is the duty of the international community as a whole to co-operate'.

English Heritage is committed to help to protect and preserve each World Heritage Site in England. We owe this not only to the world but to the people whose ancestors created them and to whom they ultimately belong.

Sir Jocelyn Stevens
Chairman, English Heritage

STONEHENGE & AVEBURY

TWO OF THE GREATEST monuments of the prehistoric world stand within thirty miles of each other on the chalk upland of Wiltshire. Avebury and Stonehenge incorporate massive upright stones that took thousands of labouring hours to erect, and each is based upon a great earthwork of encircling bank and ditch that in Avebury's case is itself one of the building achievements of the ancient world. The origins of these monuments stretch back five thousand years and more. Both stood at the centre of a variety of other monuments – mounds, earthworks, ceremonial structures, burial places and settlements – that in some cases long predate them.

The most famous of all Stonehenge's features is that it is aligned on the rising sun at midsummer. An alignment on the sun or stars was incorporated into many prehistoric ceremonial structures; unique to Stonehenge is its architectural quality. Surrounding a circle of smaller 'bluestones', brought hundreds of miles by sea from Wales, stand the carefully shaped massive sarsen upright stones with horizontal lintels on top. Enclosed within these circles are horseshoe arrangements of larger sarsen 'trilithons', pairs of uprights with a third lintel stone on top, and bluestones, all of which enclosed the originally upright Altar Stone, placed directly in line with the rising midsummer sun.

Stonehenge (below) sits in the centre of a landscape which includes monuments from all eras of prehistory. An aerial view of Stonehenge as it stands today (overleaf) clearly shows its architectural form.

The huge earth mound of Silbury Hill (above) towers over the many standing stones covering the Avebury landscape. These include the Great Circle (below centre and right) inside which the modern village is built.

Although the two monuments are situated relatively close to each other, are built of the same basic material (the super-hard sarsen sandstone), and are of broadly similar antiquity with the peak of their building activity around 2400 BC, there are also many differences. The most obvious distinction is in size: Avebury originally had 180 standing stones within an encircling bank almost a mile in circumference. The present-day village nestles within the monument, cottages and lanes set among the stones. The standing stone are largely unshaped, in contrast to Stonehenge where the circle is smaller (within a bank and ditch a hundred metres across), but in which the stones were very carefully dressed using stone tools. Although there is a larger number of ancient monuments within the Stonehenge region only vestiges of these important structures survive. The Avebury

Stonehenge is made up of an outer stone circle capped by lintels (right) with a horseshoe of larger trilithons as a focus in the centre (below right), with matching arrangements in a circle and horseshoe of the so-called bluestones, brought a huge distance from the Preseli Mountains in South Wales.

region boasts an avenue of stones to West Kennet, the great stone-built burial chamber, the West Kennet Long Barrow, Windmill Hill and, most impressive of all, Silbury Hill – the largest manmade mound in Europe, a pyramid of chalk and soil reaching to the heavens.

Stonehenge and Avebury have an importance beyond their architectural merit. They were the proving ground for British archaeology in the seventeenth and eighteenth centuries, and they continue to provide significant discoveries. Stonehenge in particular remains the focus of worship for neo-pagan cults, and both sites are objects of attraction in New Age thinking. The power these monuments have to excite, and by their size and complexity to evoke wonder at the achievements of our supposedly 'savage' and 'unsophisticated' ancestors, are unsurpassed.

The appearance of Stonehenge changes with the light, the time of day and night (below left), and from summer to winter (left).

CITY OF BATH

ACITY THAT IS A BYWORD for eighteenth-century elegance, Bath has given us words – bathchair, Bath bun – that are themselves part of its history. Much of the gentility and sophistication created in the Georgian era is still evident in a city that has long catered for the treatment of the sick. The Romans transformed a sacred Celtic site with gushing hot springs into an international attraction graced by temple and bathing complexes. Many vestiges of those buildings have been excavated; others still lie

The Classical orders of architecture were incorporated with great panache into the buildings of Georgian Bath: the grand sweep of the Royal Crescent (above and above left), the frontages of the individual houses in the Circus (opposite left) and porches and doorcases throughout the city.

beneath the streets of the modern city. Although Bath retains the bones of its medieval prosperity, in the great Abbey church and the surrounding street pattern, this is eclipsed by the novel urban planning that was begun in the 1720s and continued for a century.

Bath is unsurpassed. The ordered elegance of the baths, public buildings, squares, terraces, circuses and crescents on the hills above the original town and on the river plain is one of Europe's consummate architectural experiences. Master designers, pre-eminently John Wood (1704–54) and his son John the younger (1727–81), worked with speculative builders and landowners to make a unique resort for the gentry and aristocracy. The neo-classical purity of the Palladian architecture combined with the necessity to attract people of quality and wealth. Thus one side of Queen Square, the first of Wood's grand schemes, resembles a palace yet contains seven houses and the Circus, inspired by the Colosseum and Stonehenge, was Britain's first circular street. For many the city's crowning glory is the Royal Crescent, built by the younger Wood between 1767 and 1774.

Over a million litres of water a day gush out of Bath's hot spring, at a constant temperature of 46.5° celsius. When the Romans arrived

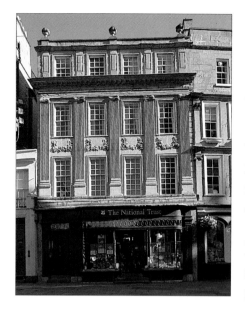

they harnessed the local cult of the deity Sul to their goddess Minerva; Bath became Aquae Sulis, and a great male gorgon's head that graced the temple pediment has survived along with a beautiful sculpted head of Minerva. These guarded the sequence of three great baths, used ever since for the curative properties of their waters. The King's Bath, above the Roman reservoir, was first built around 1100, when the city embarked on its second phase of prosperity. Bath's medieval importance is best illustrated by the abbey church, reconstructed in 1499 by Bishop King, whose dream of angels climbing ladders to heaven is recorded in stone on the west front.

The unique qualities of Bath have been recognised in the entire city being inscribed a World Heritage Site, humbler streets and buildings given their due importance alongside the great architectural set-pieces that have given it its fame.

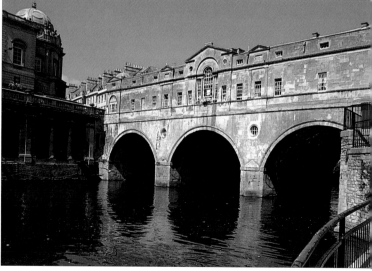

Bath's Georgian set pieces include General Wade's house (top left) and the bridges by Wood at Prior Park and by Robert Adam across the Avon (bottom left and right).

The formal interiors of the Assembly Rooms (centre left) and many private houses (centre right) emphasize the grand social position of eighteenth-century Bath.

Bath Abbey (left and above left) was one of the last great churches built before the Reformation. Its interior, graced by its fan vaulting (above), is filled with memorials which sit beside the elegant font, installed in 1710 (top).

John Wood the Younger's grand Palladian style
is shown to best effect by the Royal Crescent
Hotel, its exterior matching its neighbours.

Wood created a variety of magnificent interiors which still retain the elegance that epitomized Georgian Bath.

The waters of Bath: the Great Bath (top and opposite) had seats built in for the convenience of Roman bathers. Votive offerings were made by Roman visitors to the spa waters where the Roman-Celtic god Sul-Minerva was venerated (middle right and left). The great temple pediment was adorned by the male gorgon's head (above).

In the eighteenth century the waters were dispensed in the Georgian Pump Room (above).

CANTERBURY

The diminutive St Martin's Church (above) where St Augustine baptized King Ethelbert, contrasts with the magnificence and size of Canterbury Cathedral itself (below).

AUGUSTINE CAME TO Canterbury on his papal mission to establish Christianity in England in 597. The great and ancient churches of Canterbury that Augustine knew, founded, and where he was laid to rest, are emblematic of changes and continuities in English religious life for 1,400 years.

Three complexes of buildings form the World Heritage Site. The primary site is the cathedral of Christ Church, seat of the Primate of All England, the most senior Anglican clergyman. Nearby stand the ruins of St Augustine's Abbey, the missionary's burial place, which include the remains of three early churches that had been built end to end; and beyond that stands the little parish church of St Martin, possibly incorporating Roman remains, which was a place of Christian worship even before 597.

Of all the buildings, the cathedral is by far the most impressive. In the forefront of architectural developments throughout every period and style from the Norman of the late eleventh century to the Perpendicular of the fifteenth, Canterbury Cathedral has a grandeur

that eclipses all other churches in the land. Yet there are many domestic areas and unfinished corners within the cathedral and its precincts that add a characteristically English flourish. On the site of St Augustine's Abbey, only a few hundred metres east of the cathedral itself but originally outside the ancient city wall, there stood a row of small churches, of which only a few portions of the seventh-century church of St Pancras remain. St Augustine's became a great centre of learning before the Norman Conquest. The Norman abbots swept away much of what their predecessors had built to erect both a new church and monastic buildings on a grand scale.

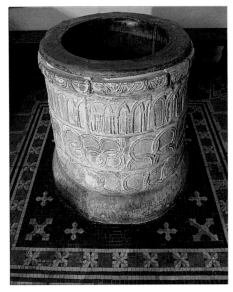

Following the abbey's dissolution in 1538, some parts were retained for a short while as a royal palace, but thereafter the site fell into ruins. St Martin's Church, further east still, incorporates Roman remains or reused materials that date back to the fourth and seventh centuries AD. This is probably the oldest continuously used Christian site in England. Bertha, Queen of Kent, was already a Christian, and it is undoubtedly the church in which she worshipped

The Norman font in St Martin's Church (above) and the ruins of St Augustine's Abbey (below).

Looking east in Canterbury Cathedral: the choir, Trinity Chapel and Corona.

even before Augustine came, and then where the missionary baptized her husband, King Ethelbert. This paved the way for the conversion of his kingdom to Christianity and then the great missionary push through England. Canterbury has remained ever since the premier focus of the nation's established religious life.

St Augustine's name was not the only great one to be associated with Canterbury. Following the brutal murder of St Thomas Becket in 1170, his tomb in the cathedral became one of England's premier places of pilgrimage, until Henry VIII's Reformation in the 1530s when the shrine and also the abbey were suppressed. When Chaucer's fourteenth-century Canterbury Pilgrims went to seek the 'holy Christian martyr' Becket, they were following a well-trodden

route between London and Canterbury. These were the twin focuses of royal and religious power: the Archbishops of Canterbury were usually among the most powerful political figures of any medieval era. Becket, murdered for his opposition to Henry II, became both saint and symbol, and an already well-endowed and artistically flourishing church increased in grandeur and importance. A succession of fires throughout the Middle Ages allowed new generations of church builders to import and adapt new architectural styles, building upon the heavy Romanesque crypt that has survived to this day.

The cathedral church is remarkable for its length, rising in level in successive stages from the nave via the crossing and choir to the Trinity Chapel, where Becket's shrine stood, and the encircling Corona at the east end. Canterbury retains the finest medieval stained glass in the country, contemporary with that at Chartres and glowing with rich colours. An impression of great height is one of the dominating features of the Perpendicular-style fourteenth-century nave, while the massive crossing tower, so-called 'Bell Harry', was one of the last major additions to the cathedral in the closing years of the fifteenth century. Moreover, as the burial place of kings and archbishops, Canterbury Cathedral contains one of the pre-eminent collections of sculpture from medieval and later times. Most famous of all is the effigy of the 'Black Prince', Edward, eldest son of Edward III, who acquired semi-legendary status in the Hundred Years War.

The great cathedral is surrounded by its former monastic buildings, some of which were later incorporated into the King's School. That combination of scales and juxtaposition of old and ancient typifies the Canterbury World Heritage Site, the cradle of English Christianity and an enduring symbol of the link between Church and State.

The cloisters of the Cathedral.

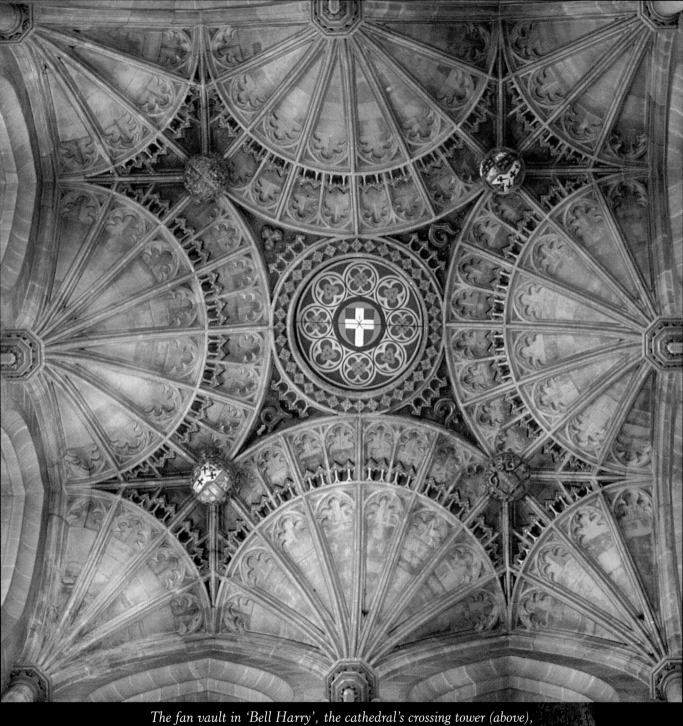

The fan vault in 'Bell Harry', the cathedral's crossing tower (above),
that rises at the eastern end of the soaring nave (opposite).

St Thomas Becket is portrayed in the medieval stained glass (above), while a stone marks
the place of his murder (above right). The cathedral's many vaulted spaces range from
the plain beauty of the Romanesque crypt (below) to the intricacy of the cloister (top)
and the great height of the nave and aisles (opposite).

Thames, the Tower was designed to subjugate a defeated and potentially troublesome population. The White Tower, the great Norman central keep 27 metres in height lies in the centre of the present complex. It was erected in stone within ten years of the first, wooden structure being built there. Succeeding monarchs extended the fortress with curtain walls, towers and gates, employing the most up-to-date military architecture to create both a palace and a stronghold. Those functions remain, although no monarch has lived there since the sixteenth century.

Yeomen Warders of the Tower

Over the centuries many famous and notorious people have lived and died within the Tower's walls. Some of those people have their own memorial. The suite of rooms in which Sir Walter Raleigh was imprisoned between 1603 and 1618 (with a two-year intermission) has been carefully reconstructed, while the oratory in which

Henry VI was murdered in 1471 can still be visited. In the chapel royal of St Peter ad Vincula, the sixteenth-century church standing close to the site of the scaffold, inscriptions record many of those put to death in Tudor and Stuart times, from Lady Jane Grey to Saints John Fisher and Thomas More. Other victims have no memorial other than the shudder with which visitors view the river entrance from the Thames, the so-called Traitors' Gate. The greatest mystery surrounds the fate of the Princes in the Tower, supposedly murdered there in 1483 by Richard III.

Of the surprisingly numerous residents in the Tower, the most distinctive are the Yeomen Warders in their red and gold uniforms. One of their number is always appointed to safeguard the ravens, the birds that live in the Tower and whose continued presence – as legend has it – guarantees the continued existence of the fortress. Ceremonial and tradition, in the form of the nightly Ceremony of the Keys, or the continued maintenance of the dazzling and rich coronation regalia of crowns, orb, sceptres and other gold and jewel-encrusted objects reaching back to the eleventh century, are integral to the Tower and its appeal.

The Tower of London, with its fortifications and collections of arms, has every semblance of a mighty military structure; it was even refortified and given much of its present appearance amid fears of revolution in the 1840s. Yet over the centuries the Tower has seen surprisingly little action – and whenever threatened by popular uprising has tended to be opened speedily to insurgents rather than suffer the indignity of attack. That survival, and its important position at the heart of the kingdom, has made the Tower of London one of the most powerful of all symbols of English royal power and the mystique of majesty.

The central keep, the White Tower (top), was begun in William the Conqueror's reign. Below it are views of some of the Tower's many corners: the gate in the Bloody Tower; the site of the scaffold on Tower Green; and Water Lane.

The might of the Tower is visible in its many gates such as the portcullis in the Bloody Tower (above left) and the notorious Traitors' Gate (above right). The might of the Normans is also integral to the magnificent Chapel of St John in the White Tower (below).

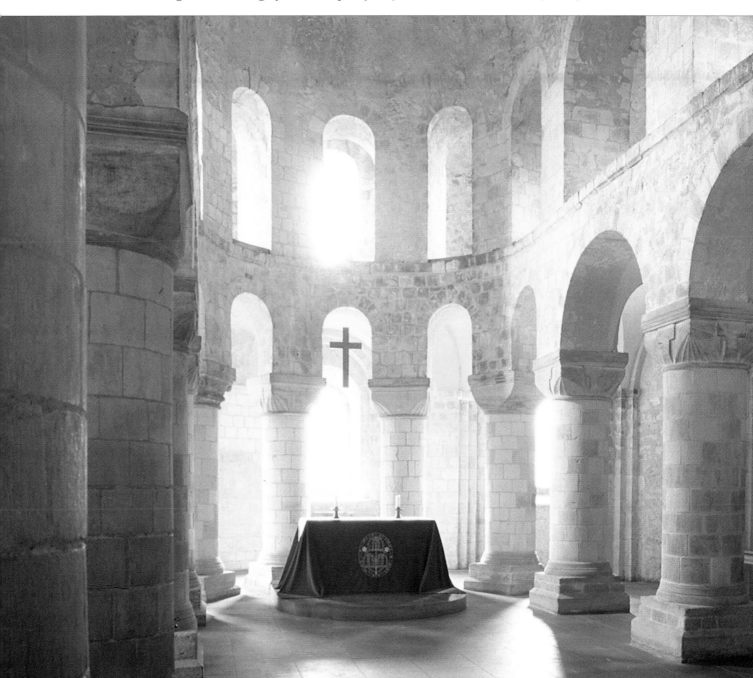

Memorials, both to those who died of natural causes (above) and at the hands of executioners (opposite), feature in the chapel royal of St Peter ad Vincula. Among those executed was Sir Walter Raleigh (left) who was imprisoned in the suite of rooms shown below between 1603 and 1616. He had fallen foul of King James VI and I, who brought the Scottish unicorn (opposite below) into the Royal coat of arms.

NEAR THIS SPOT LIE THE REMAINS OF

Lord Guildford Dudley   1554
Lady Jane Grey   1554
Henry Grey Duke of Suffolk   1554
Thomas Howard
        4th Duke of Norfolk   1572
Philip Earl of Arundel   1595
Robert Devereux Earl of Essex 1601
Sir Thomas Overbury   1613

SACRED
To the beloved Memory of
GENʳˡ CHARLES RAINSFORD
COLˡ OF THE 44ᵀᴴ REGᵀ OF FOOT
Who departed this Life
the 24ᵗʰ of May 1809
Aged 82 Years.
The most perfect Christ___
Affectionate Husband __
Fathers and sincere __
He had served Sixty __
in the Army.

GREENWICH

The process of establishing World Heritage Sites is a continuing one. Individual nations nominate new sites for consideration and ultimately for inscription on the list. It is hoped that by the end of 1997 one of the most magnificent ensembles of buildings and open spaces in England will have been welcomed officially into their company: Greenwich, on the bank of the River Thames a few miles downstream from central London.

At centre-stage are the buildings of the Royal Naval College, principally designed by Sir Christopher Wren. Their parallel forms frame Inigo Jones's Queen's House, the first wholly Renaissance building in the country, and the royal parkland beyond with the picturesque outline of the Royal Observatory (also by Wren) sitting on the skyline. All around are the elegant houses, markets and moored ships that recall Greenwich's mixed royal and maritime history.

Greenwich Palace had been a favourite of the Tudors – both Henry VIII and Elizabeth I were born within its sprawling buildings and Elizabeth's mother, Queen Anne Boleyn was arrested here.

The view of Greenwich from across the Thames (opposite) is one of the glories of the capital. Inside its buildings are the grand interiors of the Chapel (below and overleaf, left) and the Painted Hall (overleaf, right), representing respectively the neo-classical and the baroque idioms of eighteenth-century style.

Although a new palace was begun for Charles II, the present baroque buildings took shape when Mary II established the Royal Naval Hospital, a home for retired seamen, in 1692. Wren, assisted by Nicholas Hawksmoor, devised a master plan which incorporated Jones's Queen's House. It is the rhythmic space he created *between* the buildings that makes Greenwich so special, a space and vista best appreciated from the river. A great dining hall, decorated throughout by Sir James Thornhill in *trompe l'œil* glorifying the Stuarts and Hanoverians, faces a sumptuously appointed chapel, wholly refitted in 1780–88 by 'Athenian' Stuart.

The Royal Naval Hospital closed in 1869, becoming the home of the Royal Naval College. The National Maritime Museum, incorporating the Queen's House, occupies the former Royal Naval Asylum. The Queen's House, designed to straddle the road to Dover, links the palace with its royal hunting park on the other side; the Royal Observatory was established within the park in 1675, and there the prime meridian of zero degrees longitude was adopted in 1884.

The flanking streets are lined with fine houses of the seventeenth and eighteenth centuries, with fine churches by Hawksmoor and Wardell. The most tangible evidence of the trading connection is the clipper *Cutty Sark*, one-time holder of the title of fastest voyage to Sydney, Australia, built in 1869 and berthed in dry dock since 1954. Time, space and the sea are the abiding motifs of Greenwich.

Details of the Chapel's decoration with (from top) the coffered ceiling, the Royal Naval Hospital's coat of arms, and the curve of the consoles carrying the galleries. The Hospital's arms are reproduced once more on the wrought iron river entrance gates (bottom).

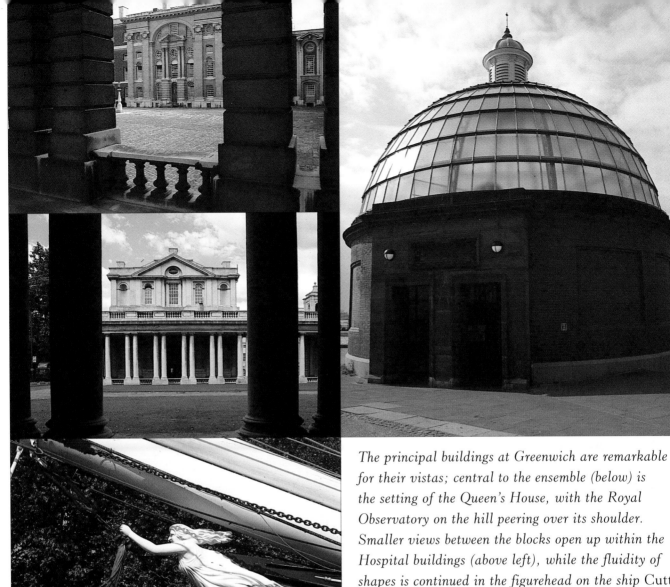

The principal buildings at Greenwich are remarkable for their vistas; central to the ensemble (below) is the setting of the Queen's House, with the Royal Observatory on the hill peering over its shoulder. Smaller views between the blocks open up within the Hospital buildings (above left), while the fluidity of shapes is continued in the figurehead on the ship Cutty Sark (left) and Greenwich's many domes. The example above crowns the entrance to the Victorian pedestrian tunnel beneath the Thames.

WESTMINSTER

THE STORY OF THE METROPOLIS is a tale of two cities: London and Westminster. The City of London stands at the ancient crossing-point of the River Thames, and it remains today the financial powerhouse of the nation. Just a couple of miles upstream is Westminster, connected by the Strand – originally, as the name implies, a sandy beach. A city in its own right, Westminster is the governmental powerhouse of the nation. Royal palace, royal church, parliament, administrative headquarters and legal centre are all concentrated within a tiny area. History, architectural grandeur and the political establishment are combined within the World Heritage Site that comprises Westminster Abbey, the Houses of Parliament (technically the Palace of Westminster), and St Margaret's church. Their joint image is one of the world's best-known sights; in their joint history the nation's story is written.

Westminster was originally Thorney Island, a swampy area beside the Thames. There are few signs of the streams and swamps today, except where archaeological excavation reveals the wooden piles and willow rafts on which some buildings were erected. St Peter's monastery, the first major building on the site, was founded only in the tenth century. Its royal connection began in the eleventh century. King Edward the Confessor, who died in 1066, established Westminster as the principal focus of royal power. The disputed succession to his throne resulted in the Norman Conquest of the same year that underwrote the central importance of Westminster.

Edward's church was rebuilt during the Middle Ages to focus upon his tomb when he had been made a saint. It is both the English coronation church and the principal royal mausoleum. It has also become the burial place of statesmen, heroes, poets and musicians. The early Norman kings used the Palace of Westminster extensively, and the earliest surviving building, Westminster Hall, dates back to the 1090s. Then the largest single room in Europe, it became the focus of royal ceremonial. During the thirteenth and fourteenth centuries the assembly at Westminster of leading courtiers and subsequently of important men from the cities and shires metamorphosed into the law-making body we know as Parliament.

The twin towers of Westminster Abbey, the tower of St Margaret's Church among the trees, and the clock tower of the Palace of Westminster, the Houses of Parliament, define the World Heritage Site. Inside the Abbey (overleaf), looking west from the choir, the nave is topped by majestic vaulting.

Only fragments remain of the original abbey church and monastery that Edward the Confessor rebuilt in the 1050s. A new abbey church was begun in 1245, largely at the expense of King Henry III who wanted to glorify his saintly royal ancestor. English kings are crowned with Edward's crown, seated in front of his shrine. Prominent members of the royal families were buried close to the Confessor. The shrine had been decorated with costly imported materials by Italian craftsmen, as was Henry's own tomb and the great pavement installed in front of the High Altar.

The abbey itself is the most French of all England's great churches, both in its soaring height and its architectural style and decoration. The eastern end of the church, the crossing and the monastery's chapter house were completed in this first great phase, at considerable cost. Henry III had to pawn some of the crown jewels to raise the finance. The nave was completed in the later fourteenth century, in conscious emulation of the style of the rest of the fabric. The grand west front remained uncompleted until the eighteenth century. In 1734 Nicholas Hawksmoor added the two west towers that are among the most familiar of all the abbey's features. Apparently Gothic in form and outline, the towers are a mixture of classical and medieval motifs. Hawksmoor also designed a cupola to crown the crossing tower, which has nevertheless remained a curiously graceless stump; the weight of any larger superstructure would have been too great for the ground conditions to bear. Although the Abbey has been restored and repaired on many occasions since, the last only just completed, the west towers were the final addition to the fabric.

Henry VII replaced the thirteenth-century Lady Chapel with a splendid and huge Perpendicular eastern extension in 1503. It was originally intended to house a shrine for Henry VI, the Lancastrian king murdered in the Tower, but his canonization never happened. Instead the chapel bears Henry VII's own name. He is buried beneath one of the greatest and most daring examples of fan vaulting, with many of his grandchildren – Edward VI, Elizabeth I and Mary Queen of Scots among them – lying in close proximity. By the time they came to be buried there, Henry VIII had begun the process of religious reformation that had swept away the old monastic way of life; since the reign of Elizabeth, Westminster has had an almost unique status as a collegiate church with a separate form of self-government. 'Abbey' is a four-century-old anachronism.

The fan vault of Henry VII's Chapel (opposite) with the banners of the Knights of the Bath, is an example of the many decorative elements in the Abbey. Its side chapels (top left) are filled with monuments, including to the Duke and Duchess of Lennox & Richmond (centre) and the infant children of James VI and I (bottom).

The Chapter House, built in 1250, contains some of the finest surviving medieval sculpture. Octagonal, with a central column, it retains its original floor of glazed tiles. At one time the seat of the House of Commons, it now houses the abbey treasures.

One of the most abiding impressions any visitor takes away from the church is of the statuary, tombs and memorials that fill almost every available surface on wall and floor, from the Tomb of the Unknown Soldier just within the west door to the tear-inducing alabaster effigy of Princess Sophia, the infant daughter of James VI and I, in her cradle away at the east. Some of the medieval royal tombs bear effigies and decoration that are among the supreme artistic achievements of their age, and exploit the special space at the eastern end. Henry V's tomb, for example, with his noble profile and a golden crown, is placed upon a special bridge connecting the ambulatory into the royal burial area. In the seventeenth century some of the most bravura – even megalomaniac – of all the Abbey's monuments were erected, with the Duke and Duchess of Lennox & Richmond's tomb the most overbearing of all.

Yet the most memorable monuments date from the eighteenth century, when artists, warriors and statesmen began to crowd the walls and aisles. L.F. Roubiliac's monuments to the Duke of Argyll, erected in 1748–8, to George Frederick Handel and J.G. Nightingale (both installed in 1761), combine great artistry and high drama.

By the nineteenth century, the tombs and monuments had become less dramatic and a political roll-call: Pitt, Peel, Disraeli and Gladstone are all remembered. The south transept has been known since the eighteenth century as Poets' Corner. Chaucer's monument was erected in 1556, and around it are the tombs and monuments of almost every major English poet and literary figure from Shakespeare to Betjeman.

The eighteenth-century stained glass from the north transept is among the best examples in the Abbey (above left). Funerary monuments of every date, from the thirteenth to the twentieth, crowd together, including Handel's (left).

Sculpture fills the narrow cloister entrance (above right) and Henry VII's Chapel (above left). Poets' Corner includes monuments to Chaucer (bottom left), the earliest, and Shakespeare (bottom right), by Scheemakers.

Frequently overlooked, yet an integral part of the Westminster setting, is the parish church of St Margaret. Although it was founded in the Norman era, most of the church's fabric dates from the start of the sixteenth century. Of the same period, but installed only in 1758, is the vast east window, brought as part of Katharine of Aragon's wedding dowry to Prince Arthur, Henry VIII's elder brother. St Margaret's church is particularly closely associated with the House of Commons in the nearby Palace of Westminster.

No monarch has lived in the palace since Henry VIII, who chose to move into Whitehall Palace just up the road. Separate Houses of Lords and Commons had been integral parts of the Parliament advising the monarch since the fourteenth century. These bodies met inside the palace. Royal justice was dispensed by the judges sitting in Westminster Hall, begun by William II in the 1090s

The Palace of Westminster (above) includes decorative elements reminiscent of the early pulpit in St Margaret's Church (left).

and remodelled in 1394–1401. The Palace of Westminster was the setting for the conflict between Charles I and Parliament that resulted in the English Civil War, and of the short-lived attempt at republicanism thereafter. The old Commons chamber witnessed the blazing oratory of Pitt and Fox. Although much of the old palace was destroyed by fire in 1834, and a new palace and separate law courts were built in Victoria's reign, Westminster's functions are still recognisably what they had become six hundred years ago.

The present Palace of Westminster is one of the grandest architectural achievements of the Victorian era. Little survived the devastating fire that engulfed the ramshackle palace buildings. The fire was itself the result of the march of progress; the wooden 'tallies' that had been the official receipts for government revenues for centuries were being systematically destroyed, but the

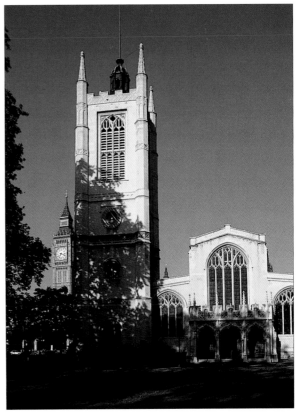

The parish church of St Margaret (right) stands between Westminster Abbey and the Houses of Parliament.

51

Barry's Palace of Westminster (above) includes a number of surviving antique portions. The great medieval Hall (below right) was built in the 1090s, and the Jewel Tower (below left) across the road once stored the royal regalia and treasures. The undercroft of St Stephen's Chapel (opposite), dating from the 1290s, also survived the fire of 1834.

conflagration got out of hand. Westminster Hall survived, together with the undercroft of St Stephen's Chapel, where the House of Commons had formerly met. An architectural competition in 1835 specifically nominated a Gothic or Elizabethan style – victory for Goths over Classicists in the nineteenth-century 'battle of the styles' – and Charles Barry won. His partner was the supreme Gothic revivalist, the young Augustus Pugin, whose intricate and sumptuous decoration fills the interior.

Barry's design for the Palace of Westminster was something of a hybrid: a rational, neo-classical skeleton, clothed in a Flemish-inspired Gothic married to Tudor Perpendicular. Nineteenth-century craving for picturesque asymmetry was assuaged by the inclusion of the two great towers, the Clock Tower (known erroneously as Big Ben, the name given to the great bell inside it) and the

Victoria Tower. The magnesian limestone that Barry specified for the structure proved to be his greatest folly, since it proved incapable of withstanding the pollution and weather of London, and has been renewed on various occasions. The building was arranged on a north-south spine, parallel to the River Thames, running from the royal apartments and the House of Lords via the Central Lobby to the House of Commons. There were also houses for the Lord Chancellor and the Speaker, with Libraries and Dining Rooms along the riverside.

The greatest single change to the Palace's structure since Barry was again through fire: enemy bombing in 1941 destroyed the House of Commons chamber. A new chamber was built in a watered-down version of the pre-existing Gothic. The dimensions of the old chamber were reproduced, although the old chamber – modelled in its turn on the undercroft of St Stephen's Chapel – had already been considered too small for its intended purpose. Not all Members of Parliament can be guaranteed a seat in a well-attended debate.

In the side of the Palace reserved for the Lords and for the Sovereign (almost exclusively when opening Parliament) Pugin's bold and colourful Gothic designs survive, and have recently been carefully restored. The Lords' Chamber, with the magnificent Royal Throne at its end, the heavily-moulded and multi-hued ceiling and the scarlet leather benches, is a riot of colour and gilding. Pugin's designs are visible throughout,

Augustus Pugin's Gothic imagination ran riot in the bedchamber (left and above right) and the staircase (right) of the Speaker's house.

down to the smallest detail; the Speaker of the House of Common's residence is one of the finest intact examples of Pugin's work and artistry.

The Palace of Westminster is not open to casual visitors, although it may be visited at a member's or peer's invitation, and access is available to debates. Situated close to the palace are the many governmental offices collectively known as Whitehall (after the palace used by Henry VIII), while the monarch's principal residence, Buckingham Palace, is still but a short carriage ride away. In Westminster, power, ceremony and majesty are intimately combined.

The area reserved for the Lords and the Sovereign is the most sumptuous part of the Palace, with the Queen's Robing Room (right and left), the Royal Gallery (centre left), vaulted and coloured corridors (above) and the House of Lords chamber (top left).

The Central Lobby (right) is the point where the Lords and Commons meet on neutral ground. Statues of eminent parliamentarians, with Winston Churchill and Lloyd George in characteristic poses, mark the entrance to the House of Commons (above left). The Members' staircase (top right) is one of the many intricate Gothic features of the interior, while in the Commons chamber itself (above) the symbol of royal authority (left) is an ever-present reminder that this remains a royal palace.

BLENHEIM PALACE

GREAT BATTLE VICTORIES often result in public commemoration. Waterloo has a railway station, Trafalgar has a square, but Blenheim has a palace. The battle of Blenheim, fought in 1704, in which England's forces were led by John Churchill, 1st Duke of Marlborough, was a signal victory in the long struggle against the might of Louis XIV and France.

The new palace which a grateful sovereign, Queen Anne, and Parliament granted to Churchill was built not as a family home but as a national monument. That fact gives the house, and the grandeur of its setting, very special qualities, and this was a palace that no royal building in Britain could match. Its titanic, highly sculpted architectural forms are themselves symbols of power and victory. The decoration continued that theme: the British lion savaging the French cock is a repeated motif, while on the south front of the house

The palace, symbol of victory over France, viewed across Capability Brown's landscaped garden and lake.

is a colossal bust of Louis XIV looking like a head set upon a stake. Inside, magnificent tapestries celebrating Marlborough's victories hang in the State Rooms alongside mementoes of his campaigns.

Ironically, many of the palace's grandest elements, inside and out, emulate Versailles. The abiding impression of the building is that it is like a stage set, with its romantic castle silhouette and receding flat planes. That can be no coincidence, since the presiding genius was the playwright-architect, Sir John Vanbrugh, magnificently supported by the highly individual skills of Nicholas Hawksmoor. Vanbrugh was one of the few architects to understand the special qualities that may be achieved by placing a building in a landscape, although his formal schemes for the grounds were soon swept away by Lawrence 'Capability' Brown. The causewayed approach that Vanbrugh had designed was part submerged to make a bridge across

the new lake, and the grass swept right up to the house. Brown's garden style, in which a 'natural' landscape was manufactured with great artifice, was one of the greatest of all English contributions to international design. Blenheim was among his masterpieces.

All this was achieved not without difficulty. Sarah, Duchess of Marlborough, who had been one of Queen Anne's favourites, fell out with her royal patron and the building funds dried up in 1711–12, and construction limped along for many years afterwards. Since the direct line had failed special arrangements for a succession to the title had to be made. Blenheim has remained the seat of one of the premier ducal families. It was here that Sir Winston Churchill, Britain's wartime Prime Minister, and regarded by many as just as great a leader as his forebear the 1st Duke, was born in 1874. The house and grounds are one of the very proudest artistic statements of a nation's gratitude for victory.

The great landscape garden by Brown was augmented in the early decades of this century by the intricate water gardens beside the West Front (below) and the Italian Garden with the Orangery Terrace beside the East Front (right, top to bottom) which were designed to enhance the immediate surroundings of the Palace.

Within the interior there are many theatrical effects: the Great Hall and proscenium arch-like entrance to the Saloon (below left) and the Chapel (left and right) with its towering monument to the first Duke and Duchess of Marlborough. Among the more domestic interiors, particular regard is given to the bedroom (below) in which Sir Winston Churchill was born.

The Library (above, left to right) is adorned with Rysbrack's statue of Queen Anne and the magnificent pipe organ. The First and Third State Rooms (left and below left), the Saloon (opposite) and many parts of the interior contain mementoes and memorials to Marlborough, including tapestries depicting his victories (below).

The theatricality of Vanbrugh's exterior (above and top right) is set off by the grand sweep of Brown's landscape (above centre), the grandiose water garden (opposite) and garden sculptures and buildings.

IRONBRIDGE

GIVEN THE SEEMING TRANQUILLITY of the River Severn as it flows through its wooded gorge in central Shropshire, it is often difficult to imagine this as a region of heavy industry amid the onset of the 'industrial revolution', arguably Britain's greatest gift to the world. There are none of the 'dark satanic mills', the tall chimneys and disciplined factory labour forces that are usually associated with industrialization. Yet throughout the eighteenth century this was one of the primary industrial areas in England; industrial activity continued here until well within living memory. Coalbrookdale – one of the streams that feeds into this part of the Severn – is known throughout the world as the place in which iron was first smelted using coke, rather than charcoal or coal with their impurities.

Although this area is often hailed as 'the cradle of the industrial revolution', that title could be given to many other parts of Britain as the eighteenth century progressed and the economy began its seemingly continuous pattern of growth. Many of those areas shared certain characteristics with the Severn gorge: ready water supplies for power, woodland for charcoal, easily available raw materials (here iron, limestone, bitumen and coal), and an adaptable labour force attracted by the lack of controls on their movement and the availability of spare land on which to build.

What made this area special was the technical energies and inventiveness of a few leading people, and the supreme emblem of the achievement of their industry, the iron bridge spanning the Severn that gives this section of the river its name. Built in 1777–81 (by Abraham Darby III, the grand-son of Abraham Darby who had first smelted iron using coke), this was the world's first major bridge made in cast iron: it must have seemed barely credible when it was constructed. The bridge is the embodiment of the 'heroic' age of industrial change. Iron rails and wheels for wagon-roads were among the area's other innovations in the eighteenth century, as well as an iron barge built on the Severn in 1787; with its links into the extensive canal network, the Ironbridge area remained important as an iron-producing centre until well into the nineteenth century.

The Severn gorge was spanned by the innovative iron bridge in 1777.

Only a couple of miles in length, the region designated the World Heritage Site incorporates a wealth of different industrial relics, in iron production and in other trades. Often rescued from near-dereliction over the past twenty-five years, the sites include other important bridges over the Severn and its tributaries, the canal, warehouses and wharves that vary from the prosaic in design to the bizarre, furnaces, a steam-powered lift, and the Tar Tunnel – a mine's drainage shaft which was found to be an ideal collection point for natural bitumen. In addition to heavier industry, the Ironbridge region was noted in the nineteenth century for some more decorative industries. Coalport china is still highly regarded; the Jackfield area

The iron bridge itself is reflected in the waters of the River Severn.

housed two of the country's largest producers of decorative Victorian ceramic tiles.

Today many of the industrial monuments have been turned into one of the nation's most thriving open air museums. There are also the houses and public buildings that sprang up on the banks of the Severn, from the irregularly-constructed cottages of the seventeenth and eighteenth centuries to the grander ironmasters' houses, the chapels, workhouse and meeting rooms of the late Georgian and Victorian years. Away from the great industrial cities, a highly significant chapter of Britain's, indeed the world's, industrial story is encapsulated in this short section of the Severn valley.

The variety of Ironbridge's industrial activities (anti-clockwise from top) that is now preserved: the delicacy of the bridge's detailing, the early steam-driven beam engine, the 1840 'Gothic warehouse' beside the Severn, the living history of the open-air museum, the Coalport china works and Victorian iron furnaces.

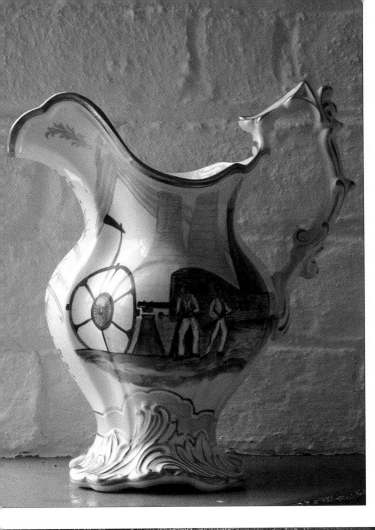

Coalport china and other decorative artefacts, celebrating the achievements of the building of the iron bridge and the region's other industrial innovations.

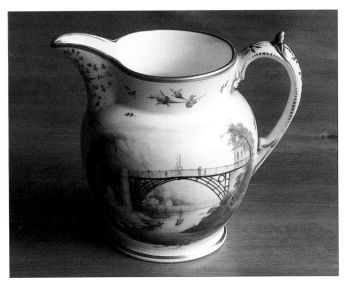

FOUNTAINS ABBEY & STUDLEY ROYAL

ONE OF THE FEW GREAT eighteenth-century 'green gardens' to have survived more or less in its original form, Studley Royal was the creation of the Aislabie family who had retreated to the wildness of their Yorkshire estate to escape financial scandal in 1720. The Aislabies incorporated into their garden scheme one of England's most glorious monastic ruins, Fountains Abbey. Ironically, the Abbey had also been founded in this secluded valley of the River Skell by monks who broke away from their mother house in York, to escape its scandal and laxity. Each principal element in the World Heritage Site, garden and abbey ruin, is magnificent in itself; together, the effect is sublime. The view of the abbey is engineered as a 'surprise' at the end of the intended route through the garden: one eighteenth-century visitor could but exclaim, 'Oh! What a beauty and perfection of ruin!!'

Fountains Abbey church, the east end seen from the garden of Studley Royal (below) and set among its monastic buildings (above right). Of those buildings, the west range is the proudest survivor (below right).

Described as a place 'more fit for wild beasts than men to inhabit' when the monks arrived in 1132, Fountains offered a sheltered valley and water. Adopted into the Cistercian order, Fountains Abbey thrived, becoming a great land-owner whose farming wealth was reflected in the variety and extent of its buildings, that nevertheless still reflected the simple ideals of its foundation.

The ruins of the abbey, which was dissolved by Henry VIII in 1539, include the roofless shell of the proud abbey church. The west range of monastic buildings has survived remarkably intact, a great length of vaults springing from a central row of pillars. Substantial portions of the chapter house, cloister and many of the domestic buildings also remain. The monks lived a life of rigorous austerity within buildings that were adorned by little other than their own simple beauty. After the foundation was dissolved, the buildings were a useful quarry for building material for the new owners of the estate; Sir Stephen Proctor used stone from the abbey to build Fountains Hall, a

The east guest house (top left) and chapter house entrance (opposite top) are both preserved within the Fountains Abbey complex, which now stands within Studley Royal's gardens. The gardens (centre left, below left and below right) feature temples and statues around geometrically-shaped ponds, set against a dark background of trees, their formality contrasting with the open sweep of deer park (centre right).

mellow and romantic house begun in 1598 to designs attributed to Robert Smythson, the builder of Hardwick Hall.

This portion of the estate was bought in 1767 by the neighbouring Aislabies as the culmination of their grand garden scheme. John Aislabie had become Chancellor of the Exchequer in 1717; but in 1721, as one of the promoters of the notorious South Sea Bubble, he was forced to resign from parliament. Work had already begun on the gardens at Studley Royal, but now he threw himself fully into the garden schemes. The River Skell was channelled into a series of geometrically-cut ponds and water features, ending in a great lake beside the old deer park, and the valley sides were planted with trees, especially evergreens that gave the garden all-year-round interest. Statuary, temples and pavilions were all integral features of the design, culminating in the view of the abbey ruins. The gardens subsequently decayed, but they were never swept away and, now restored, are a remarkable and a precious survival.

Although the Aislabies' house burned down in 1946, one further great building survives: St Mary's Church, built in 1871–8. It is the ecclesiastical masterpiece of William Burges, one of the greatest Gothic Revival architects. The interior is filled with colour and decoration, the exterior designed in a mixture of medieval styles – all wholly different from both garden and abbey, yet just as much an individual and precious marvel as either of them.

*Fountains Hall (top left) was built from 1598 using stone taken from the abbey ruins. At
the other end of the estate, by contrast, St Mary's Church (top right) embodies a renewed
Victorian piety. The rich interior (opposite and above right) was designed down to the finest detail by
William Burges for the Marquess and Marchioness of Ripon, who were buried within it (above left),
as a memorial to their son who had been killed in Greece.*

DURHAM

URHAM, AVIGNON and Prague are cities sharing the distinction of buildings in dramatic settings that jointly express military might and ecclesiastical power. Stronghold and cathedral stand together. Of the three, the drama is greatest at Durham: the castle in which the former prince-bishops lived, who ruled like kings over the county palatine, and the cathedral in which they were en-throned, stand side by side above steep sandstone cliffs, impregnable on a virtual island in the River Wear. Being built of the same stone, castle and cathedral almost seem to grow out of the cliffs; the sight from below is one of the world's great vistas. Yet neither castle nor cathedral would have had the power they embodied in the Middle Ages – and were able to maintain even until the early nine-teenth century – were it not for a self-effacing holy man who had hidden himself away on the Farne Islands, off the Northumberland coast. From 995 the Benedictine monastery at Durham, which later formed the basis of the cathedral, was the last resting place of St Cuthbert, who had died in 685 and whose remains were later carried around the north-east in flight from the invading

Durham Cathedral (left) towers above the River Wear in an impregnable position. The might of its internal structure is counterbalanced by the lightness of the innovative rib-vault roof (opposite).

Vikings. His tomb became one of the great pilgrimage centres of northern Christendom.

In the years that followed the Norman Conquest the bishops of Durham assumed many quasi-royal legal and military powers to rule within the county. The castle, with its mighty Norman structure overlaid by many different architectural features and styles, was the bishops' principal official residence for over seven centuries until it was given to form the new University of Durham in 1836. The Norman chapel, galleries and intricately-carved portals still form the building's skeleton, however much it may have been adorned by later ecclesiastical dignitaries. Perhaps the most significant was Bishop Cosin, who after the Restoration in 1660 spent vast sums on repairing and adorning both castle and cathedral. The woodwork he commissioned is especially memorable: the 'Black Staircase' cantilevered from the castle walls, and the cathedral's soaring font cover and choir stalls.

The power of the Normans is best expressed in the cathedral, that stands across the lawns of Palace Green from the castle. Mighty cylindrical columns bear the structure's weight, their bulk deliberately reduced by incising them with deep-cut

The clock in the north transept (above) was the only wooden fitting to escape destruction when Scottish prisoners were incarcerated in the cathedral during the Civil War. The Victorian restorations included the marble-inlaid pulpit and intricate pavements (left).

patterns – flutes, spirals, zig-zags. Most innovative, though, was the cathedral's incorporation for the very first time of rib vaulting in the roofs, harbinger of the Gothic building style that superseded the Romanesque of the Normans. The vaults brought a new lightness to the building's mass; perhaps here they also recall the branches tied to make the first covering for Cuthbert's coffin.

Cuthbert still lies in his tomb behind the high altar, with the vast Chapel of the Nine Altars beyond. Fragments of his wooden coffin, exquisite thousand-year-old embroidered burial vestments, and the saint's jewelled cross are the most precious items in the cathedral's possession. The great saint and historian Bede (who died in 735) lies in a tomb within the Lady Chapel, or Galilee, a structure standing high above the cliff edge at the cathedral's west end. The saints' graves survived the terrible destruction of the cathedral's furnishings and treasures in both the Reformation and the Civil War.

A steep pathway up the densely-wooded slope emerges directly beneath the west front, and reaches the plateau between castle and cathedral. No attacker ever succeeded in that climb, to one of the architectural treasures of the world.

The massiveness of the Norman columns was reduced by their surface decoration (right). Illuminated manuscripts are among the cathedral's surviving glories and include depictions of St Cuthbert with the head of St Oswald (centre right). A lighter medieval touch is evident in the choir, seen from high up in the crossing (top right).

Zig-zag patterns were brought into exuberant play in the Galilee, or Lady Chapel (overleaf).

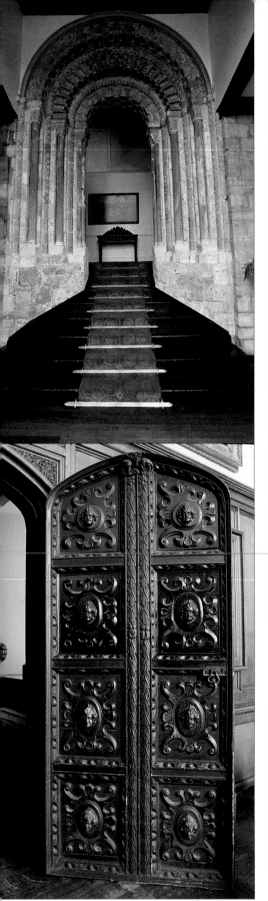

*Seventeenth-century carvings adorn the entrance to the hall in the Castle (above left),
and the cantilevered staircase in the main domestic block (centre right). The castle's later
fabric still contains powerful reminders of its medieval past: the entrance doorway from
the courtyard (top right), and the Norman chapel (above right and opposite).*

HADRIAN'S WALL

T HE MOST IMPRESSIVE piece of military engineering in the ancient world, Hadrian's Wall was built across the narrow neck of England in Cumbria and Northumberland to guard the Roman empire against the unconquerable Scots. In the second century AD the emperor Hadrian, one of the shrewdest of all the great rulers of Rome, marked the edges of the Roman world with physical boundaries, running across north Africa, the Middle East, eastern and northern Europe, and so reversed the ever-expansionist policies of his predecessors in favour of consolidation and limitation.

His mighty wall snakes for over seventy miles from the River Tyne in the east to the Solway Firth in the west, with additional protection along the coast of Cumbria. In the wild and little-inhabited central portion, substantial sections remain visible today. Many parts of the wall and its attendant sites within the military zone are remarkably well-preserved, which, through archaeological investigations conducted since the eighteenth century, have provided an almost unparalleled picture of army life on the edge of empire.

The three hooded deities, the genii cucullati (below), whose image recurs throughout the region, guarded the soldiers on the often bleak and open wall, seen here at Hotbank Crag (opposite).

The museum of excavated artefacts at Chesters fort displays statues of Roman and local gods and goddesses (left), as well as a water god (top) and the figure of Juno (below), together with a bronze measure for a soldier's grain ration (below left).

The wall at Cawfields stretches across the bleak Northumbrian countryside (overleaf).

Along the stone wall (still over a metre high in some places) run the parallel lines of the defensive bank and ditch on the northern side and the ditch and banks of the *vallum* on the south. The wall was built with milecastles at intervals of a Roman mile (slightly less than a modern mile) with guarded turrets between them a third of a mile apart. The wall was never intended to act as an impenetrable barrier against the barbarian hordes, but as a semi-permeable frontier, with the soldiers supervising traffic across it, although they were also able to close the wall at a moment's notice or to range well into Scotland.

Very soon after the wall was built, between 122 and 138 AD, the decision was made to strengthen it and move the forts in which the thousands of soldiers guarding the border resided from the wall's hinterland up onto the wall itself. The excavated forts at Housesteads and Chesters provide ample evidence for the conditions in which the Roman soldiers lived. The commanding officer usually had a substantial house, while his men lived in close-set barracks. Temples soothed their spirits, granaries were provided to store their food, while the men's comforts were not forgotten: there were latrines, scoured by running water, and substantial bath-houses incorporating hot baths and steam rooms with under-floor heating systems.

Thus the surroundings may have seemed bleak, but a cold, wet soldier coming off duty would have had some possibility of relaxation. In these forts, and at Vindolanda a little south of the wall itself, excavation has uncovered many other aspects of the garrison's way of life.

Survivals from Roman times include a remarkably well-preserved leather shoe (below).

The stone that was quarried at the sites provided most of the structures of the wall, from the pillars used for ventilation of the granaries at Housesteads fort (above) to the massive length of Hadrian's Wall itself, as seen, for example, at Walltown Crags (right).

There are carved effigies of their gods, including the figure of Fortuna who helped give the soldiers luck as they gambled in the baths, and the three hooded deities, the *genii cucullati*, wrapped up like soldiers against the wind and the rain. The houses were adorned with statuary, and in some instances window glass. Personal artefacts survive, especially at Vindolanda where damp conditions have preserved much organic material, including wooden tablets bearing writing, pens, shoes, locks and keys. Some of the remains of the wall are now in built-up areas of Newcastle and its environs, but much of it is still in bleak open countryside (perhaps even barer now than when the Romans were here), mute testimony to the great empire the Romans built and then slowly abandoned as their world crumbled.

Parnesius, the centurion in Rudyard Kipling's *Puck of Pook's Hill*, said, 'Old men who have followed the Eagles since boyhood say nothing in the Empire is more wonderful than the first sight of the Wall.' Modern visitors who come upon it can but echo that sentiment.

ACKNOWLEDGEMENTS

"I would like to thank all those who made this book possible in such a short time."

This book photographed and designed for English Heritage by John Hedgecoe. With grateful thanks to the publishers, Collins & Brown, and especially to Mark Collins, Colin Ziegler, Robin Gurdon and Claire Graham.

ENGLISH HERITAGE
Sir Jocelyn Stevens;
June Prunty; Katherine Thomas

BLENHEIM
Blenheim Palace
His Grace The Duke of Marlborough;
Paul Duffie

CANTERBURY
Canterbury Cathedral
Lieutenant-Colonel D.P. Earlam

St Augustine's Abbey
Peter Mills

St Martin's Church
The Revd Peter Mackenzie;
Mary Lawrence

DURHAM
Durham Cathedral
The Very Revd John Arnold;
Paul Whittaker; John McGowan

Durham Castle
A.E. Cartmell

FOUNTAINS ABBEY & STUDLEY ROYAL
Martin Drury; Terry Frazier

TOWER OF LONDON
Major-General G.M. Field;
Major Hugh Player

WESTMINSTER
Chapel of St Mary Undercroft
Canon Grey

House of Commons
Peter Jennings; Philip Wright;
Air Vice Marshall David Hawkins

House of Lords
Mary Morgan; Polly-Ann Lawson

Westminster Abbey
Dr Wesley Carr; Emma St. John-Smith

St Margaret's Church
The Revd Dr D.C. Grey

CITY OF BATH
Tony du Sautoy; Stephen Bird
Ross Stevenson – The Royal Crescent Hotel

IRONBRIDGE
Glen Lawes; Katie Foster; Glenys Espley

HADRIAN'S WALL
Dr Chris Young; Karen Parker

STONEHENGE & AVEBURY
Clews Everard – English Heritage
Celia Mead – National Trust

GREENWICH
Royal Naval College
Commander J.M.C. Maugham
Lt Anna Wright